Land Moo-la

"How Land can be Your Cash Cow"

By: Brian Patton, CCIM

101 Tips to Sell Your Land Faster & For More Moo-la

From the author of the *"Mailbox Moo-la, How Real Estate Cash Cows Put Money in Your Mailbox"* Series of books.

Forward

In Brian's first popular book, <u>Mailbox Moo-la, How Real Estate Cash Cows Put Money In Your Mailbox</u>, he focused on the seven years of investing that lead him to support himself and his family solely from the income produced by his rental properties. At the young age of 37, he retired from the day- to-day grind of a 9-5 job.

The book received acclaim from his peers.   It was recommended as a "must read" in *Commercial Investment Real Estate Magazine*, distributed by the CCIM Foundation, highlighted in Georgia Realtor magazine, and is available on Amazon.

In his book, a special "Commercial Edition" of <u>Mailbox Moo-la,</u> Brian used his years of representing commercial landlords and tenants, selling multi-family housing, and working development deals to simplify the language of commercial real estate. His conversational style of writing made for an easy read and simplified the commercial and development process for newbies and experts alike.

In this, his latest book, Brian uses his experiences as a top real estate broker in the Atlanta Georgia area, a land planner, zoning expert, and a former city planner, to help sellers and buyers with the most difficult real estate transactions on the planet...land sales. Land deals can take many months...and sometimes years...to get to the closing table. Even after they are under contract, the speed of getting a contract to the closing table will test the patience of the most experienced seller.

But, if you are persistent and do some initial work, you can use some of Brian's personal experiences to make the closing of a land deal a little easier. Whether you are a buyer or seller, with proper advice, land ownership can be some of the most financially rewarding transactions you will ever experience.

This publication is designed to provide general information regarding the subject matter covered. However, laws and practices often vary from state to state and are subject to change. Because each factual situation is different, specific advice should be tailored to the particular circumstances. For this reason, the reader is advised to consult with his or her own advisor regarding that individual's specific situation.

The author has taken reasonable precautions in the preparation of this book and believes the facts presented in the book are accurate as of the date it was written. However, neither the author nor the publisher assumes any responsibility for any errors or omissions. The author and publisher specifically disclaim any liability resulting from the use or application of the information contained in this book, and the information is not intended to serve as legal or tax advice related to individual situations.

Table of Contents

Zoning & Land Use

1. Make Zoning Work In Your Favor.
Zoning is the body of law that encompasses the rights and privileges granted by a local jurisdiction for the legally allowed use of the property. Little, if anything, affects your value more than Zoning...to the good or bad.

As a former zoning administrator for 12 years in two different jurisdictions near Atlanta, Georgia, I've seen the benefits and the damages zoning laws can produce. As a believer in limited government control, I view zoning as a "necessary evil."

As an investor, I prefer to purchase property that is in an area with strong zoning regulations for several reasons:

Strict zoning laws help maintain property values.

I personally have purchased properties in a jurisdiction that is known for strong code enforcement, specifically Alpharetta, Georgia, a suburb of Atlanta. A code enforcement officer can normally see a problem, knock on the door, and the problem is resolved in a few days.

An effective code enforcement officer is like having your own maintenance man running around with a gun and badge requiring your tenants to keep the place clean. That's a valuable service that I take advantage of anytime I can.

One particular code enforcement officer that I know has been a huge asset to me He keeps an eye on the community and keeps it cleaned up.

An occasional phone call from him about an erosion problem, downed trees, etc. will also get me off my duff and correct the problem. Befriend your local code enforcement guy, and he will be a valuable asset for you in your constant battle against maintenance problems.

Strong zoning laws tend to regulate the supply and demand market cycles. A community with strong zoning laws usually has a lot of obstacles for developers to overcome in order to start developing. As a developer, I obviously haven't liked this part of government control. But as an investor, it helps to protect the status quo.

This government control decreases your competition by increasing what we call "barriers to entry." This barrier actually helps preserve and protect your land value.

The jurisdiction will require numerous public meetings, require ad nauseam permitting meetings, and will generally put the developer through a hair-pulling-out process before he can build more real estate. It is this slow process that makes it hard to develop in most communities, and this slow process will be to your advantage as an owner of existing land.

2. Keep up with Sewer Plans for your County. Access to public sewer can greatly increase the value of your property; especially if your property is desirable for a residential subdivision or a commercial development. Even if your property is a half-mile away from sewer, sometimes it can still **be beneficial for a developer to gain access for sewer to** your property.

3. Know The Zoning Code Better than They Do.

Do existing zoning laws allow you to do what you want with the property? Here's a word to the wise. **Don't just pick up the phone and call the local jurisdiction to ask a question.** Take it from a former insider. I can tell you there's a lot of misinformation that is given out to the public.

For instance, I recently purchased a building lot and had a mobile home that I wanted to put on the property. The mobile home was a small 45' mobile home in pretty good shape that was built in 1983. I went to the county where I was putting the mobile home in order to purchase a permit. As I'm applying for the permit, the county planner looks over my application with a critical eye.

"Oh, sir, you can't move this mobile home into the county because it was built before 1988." Now, I knew she was wrong – the date was actually 1979. I had done my homework prior to filling out the application.

So, I replied that I thought that she was incorrect. With a very sharp tone, she advised me that she wasn't and that she wouldn't process my application.

So, what to do? I don't know if she purposely told me the wrong information or if it was a simple mistake. But, I had to leave and come back when someone else was manning the permit window. I eventually got my permit and moved the mobile home onto the property.

The bottom line is that you have to know the zoning code better than the planners.

It's a lot of work, but it can cost you a lot of money if you don't. I know you shouldn't have to. People should do their job, but sometimes they don't. You have to be proactive to make sure that you protect your interests.

Not long after I left one of the local zoning jurisdictions to start my real estate company, I received a call from a real estate agent with interest in one of my listings that was in the same jurisdiction. She wanted to know the zoning on the property, and she wanted to know if a restaurant would be allowed on the property. I assured her that the existing zoning did allow the restaurant.

After a few days of not hearing from her, I made a follow-up call to see if we could make a deal happen. The deal was dead in her opinion because she had called the zoning department and one of the planners told her that a restaurant wouldn't be allowed. I assured her that information was incorrect.

She continued to argue with me until I insisted that I was right because I had helped write the zoning code in question. I sent her a copy of the appropriate section of the code to prove that her client could operate a restaurant in our building. She finally believed me, but the misinformation probably cost us a deal. Her client had found somewhere else that he liked better and our window of opportunity had been closed. Know the code.

4. Don't forget Flag Lots. A flag lot is just what it sounds like...a lot shaped like a flag. In most jurisdictions, this kind of lot is still allowed. It helps in creating usable lots in the rear of your property.

Some properties are oddly shaped, and this can negatively affect the value. **But, the use of flag lots can help resolve that issue.**

5. Know About Grandfather Status

Your existing zoning research should include checking all laws pertaining to your property. This is usually in the form of one book that you can purchase or find on the jurisdiction's website. **It is important to keep a copy of this book.** It would be even better to have the copy certified and dated by someone in the local government… sometimes this is the city clerk, the mayor, a commissioner, or the jurisdiction's attorney. The reason you should keep a copy is to have evidence of any "non-conforming use" status, which is sometimes called "grandfather status."

Jurisdictions change laws all the time; and most of the time, if your use is legal, then any subsequent changes to the zoning law would provide a clause that allows you to continue that use. This is what is referred to as "grandfather status." It might even be the shape of your land parcel, or building setbacks on your property. For instance, sometimes flag lots are prohibited in new zoning codes. If your lot is a flag lot, it would become non-conforming but would have the "grandfathered status." You must keep this in mind and keep documentation of it. Know the zoning law. Know your rights. And document both.

6. Get Your Future Zoning by Getting Your Future Land Use Designation

Most jurisdictions have comprehensive land use plans that are updated every few years. In the State of Georgia, this is mandated by the state for local governments of a particular size (which is most of them). Inside this document is usually a "future land use plan." **This future land use map shows each individual property in the jurisdiction and the future land use that the local government envisions for the property.**

I have purchased several properties simply because this plan shows that the future use is office or some other type of commercial development, but the property wasn't priced accordingly. The jurisdiction uses this plan to help guide them on future zoning changes.

Perhaps your property is a small house with land on a major roadway that is transitioning from residential to commercial. Even if it's still zoned for agricultural or residential use, the future land use plan may indicate that it should be an office someday. This will give you great ammunition and some legal standing for a zoning change in the future if you so desire.

If you want to get a leg up on future zoning changes for your property, then you should contact the government planning office to see when the next future land use plan change will be considered.

Often, these meetings are much less controversial than the public hearings held for zoning changes.   And while they are open to the public, they rarely draw much attention from the public.

If you can make a case for it, the municipality may change the "future land use designation" on your property without much problem. This is the first step in the re-zoning process, and often the government leaders welcome public input in this process.

7. Rezone the Land Yourself with the aid of a zoning attorney. I've
seen many deals fall apart because the rezoning politics change over time. If rezonings are easy in your jurisdiction, go ahead and rezone before you find a buyer. One client we had gave up a rezoning that

was already in the works and about to be approved, for 50 residential lots on his property. The developer, who was also the applicant, bailed out on him on the deal and the owner didn't continue the zoning case. Months later, he was struggling to get 35 lots approved in rezoning on the same property. **If you wait, you might not be able to get the same zoning density.**

There are some risks to this strategy.

Number one, your land value will improve, and your property taxes will probably increase.

Secondly, it's very likely that your new zoning plan won't match a buyer's criteria. However, the ability to cement a higher density zoning might outweigh the pitfalls.

8. Make sure You, the landowner, are the Applicant on a Rezoning.

To reiterate the lesson learned from our client mentioned in the above scenario, make sure you are the applicant in the rezoning; and most importantly, **have the right to continue the rezoning application** if the developer / builder drops out. Get this in writing from the local zoning jurisdiction, preferably from the city/county attorney…with the aid of your rezoning attorney.

9. Subdivide before the Zoning Code Changes. In the same vane as above, **zoning laws can change dramatically and quickly.** I've seen agricultural lot minimums go from one acre to 10 acres with the swipe of a pen from a local government. If your property is suited for one acre agricultural lots, consider subdividing now. It's an easy process. Just hire a local surveyor and contract with them to subdivide and plat the property.

It's usually even easier to "re-combine" the tracts at a later date if you want. So, there's not a lot of risks...but verify it with a qualified professional.

10. Make Sure Development Trends are in Your Favor All real estate has a certain lifecycle. A Realtor friend of mine shared this analogy with me: The lifecycle of real estate is like the face of a clock. At 12:00 the property is born, at

3:00 it begins a growth cycle, at 6:00 stabilization, at 9:00 decline and blight, and rebirth at 12:00. A lifecycle may be around two or three years up to twenty years. Many urban areas go through multiple rebirthings. Figuring out where an area is in its lifecycle is extremely important. It's best to purchase the property at the beginning of the growth cycle – 3:00.

Aerial maps of your investment area from years ago will show the growth that the area has undergone, indicating particular directions and along which specific paths real estate has grown. Within this area, land uses have probably changed from agricultural and residential to office, retail, and higher density residential. This is the natural progression of development, and you should familiarize yourself with these trends. **Your job as an investor or land owner will be to read these trends and understand how they affect your real estate value.**

Most American cities grew around transportation corridors, some even beginning from Native American trails and trading posts. Transportation plays a major role in community growth trends. For instance, rail transportation was the impetus for American city growth. Hence, most manufacturing activities were located around rail facility hubs.

Downtown locations were important because businesses had to be close together to conduct business. Before fax machines and email, the attorney's office had to be close to the accountant and real estate office out of necessity.

Failure to predict a city's growth cycle can result in disaster. For instance, Japanese investors in the 1980's poured huge amounts of money into U.S. real estate only to discover that they had purchased during the top of the cycle. Subsequently, they lost a huge amount of equity and capital.

On a local level, a friend of mine owned a 15,000 square-foot retail building on the northern boundary of a community with quickly changing demographics. It was surrounded by new car lots. But, the changing demographics didn't bode well for him. This particular demographic were not purchasers of new cars. Being a mostly low-income immigrant class, they relied heavily upon mass transportation and inexpensive used cars. My friend, seeing this trend coming, put his property on the market to sell.

A local investor decided to buy the property. You would think he would understand demographic changes, but apparently, he didn't. To make matters worse, he purchased the property about six months prior to the failure of several car companies (and subsequent federal bailout) in early 2009. Several of the car dealerships closed creating a wasteland of weeds and asphalt, right next door to where he was trying to attract retailers and restaurants. Subsequently, within a matter of six months the new owner had lost every tenant; and soon after that, lost the property to foreclosure.

Of course, that doesn't mean this property will be totally abandoned. Most likely the bank will write down the loss on the property until the value reaches equilibrium. This equilibrium will be determined by the prevailing market rents. And, those rents will be determined by the tenants that are eventually attracted to the area because of the demographics. The reduction in the rent, which I predict will be from 50-65%, will subsequently reduce the value of the property by the same amount.

Failure to understand this life cycle of cities led to several people losing a lot of money, including the bank.

The bottom line is to know when to sell and when to hang on based upon demographic changes in your area.

11. Attend local government rezoning meetings regularly. Many

buyers and developers are regular attendees at local rezoning meetings. **You can hang out and talk** with rezoning attorneys, developers, and land owners...all of which are regulars. You can also get a pulse on what the local jurisdiction is approving, or denying, in land rezonings.

12. Roads, Sprawl & the Vocal Locals. Sprawl is the four letter word of

community planning. Sprawl is the expansion of development that increases demand on transportation and services which are difficult to fund and properly deal with by encouraging development in fringe areas.

This sprawl is often a by-product of zoning laws not allowing higher densities. The developer, not being able to build a product that is affordable to his target market, has to move where land prices are cheaper. Land prices are cheaper in the fringe areas – areas further away from the city center. So, his target market moves to the fringe area and drives into the city center, increasing traffic congestion, long commutes, and pollution.

If higher density were allowed closer to the city center, then the land costs per unit would be decreased, and the developer could provide affordable products for his target market.

There seems to be a disconnect between what the American public wants and what they say they want. Most developers that try to provide a higher density product with a mix of uses, such as housing, office, retail, and restaurants, find strong, vigilant, and organized opposition from the public.

I've been in many zoning hearings where the public was up in arms about projects that eventually were approved and were wildly successful. The "vocal locals" as I call them usually come out in force to intimidate the decision makers. While I agree sometimes the developer may need to be reigned in; we also must understand the capital real estate markets. The developer, hopefully, is providing something of value. If he doesn't, he'll go bankrupt.

The tip here is that the "vocal locals" may negatively affect your property values. Be cognizant of their politics and be prepared. **It might benefit you to meet with their leadership to find out what their hot buttons are.** That way you can prepare for their inevitable concerns, and properly address them during any rezoning or permitting processes.

13. Subdivide your property. You can hire a surveyor who knows the local regulations to subdivide the property. Larger tracts are sometimes harder to sell...fewer buyers since it's more expensive. But consider selling smaller tracts, for a **higher price per acre** to find more qualified buyers.

Physical Improvements

14. Watch New Sewer Projects for Re-routing options. It might be possible to have sewer lines re-routed closer to your property; especially if the sewer engineers are having trouble obtaining easements from other owners. **Offer your property as an option** and indicate that you will be really easy to work with.

15. Ask for Sewer Taps. If sewer engineers are planning on installing sewer lines through your property, then it would be a good time to ask for sewer taps or new sewer lines to more remote parts of your property. The value of this improvement might be more than being paid cash for the sewer easement, so you should weigh that option.

16. Hook up to County Water, if you can. If you have an opportunity to tap into county water, do it.

I have well water and county water. I especially love well water, **but most buyers are going to want publicly maintained water** for safety reasons. Keep both, if possible.

17. Have a Soil Survey prepared for a Septic system. If you don't have access to public sewer, then your option will be a private septic system. Most counties require a soil survey for these systems. Some counties will require a percolation test...where holes are dug, and water is poured in. If it percolates at an acceptable rate, then your septic should. **Find out what your county requires,** and have this report prepared, so a potential buyer knows what he's getting.

18. Planting trees can add value. If the land is flat and open, planting trees can not only add privacy but beauty as well. Make sure that when you plant the trees,

their placement does not block any scenic views that your property offers. Also, consult with an arborist in your area to determine the best trees to plant. Always **consider the mature size of the tree** and plan accordingly.

Trees will do more than just add beauty and privacy. They will also add significant value. The value of timberland continues to rise each year and often offers a higher return than stocks. In addition, landowners can take advantage of tax benefits if they own timberland.

19. Planting trees can also diminish value.

Many jurisdictions have specimen tree buffer requirements ...meaning, if you have some large diameter trees on the property, you can't build around them. Sometimes, this buffer extends beyond the tips of the branches. I've seen several **developments stopped, and properties remain on the market for years** because of this buffer requirement. Obviously, it could be many years before your newly planted trees become "specimens." But, you could be creating a "growing" problem. Rural areas seldom have these regulations. But, it definitely could become a problem in urban areas (and those becoming more urbanized). So, watch out.

20. Build a structure, such as a
hunting cabin or pole barn. While this isn't an improvement that's affordable or practical for every piece of land, it's something to be considered – **especially if you plan on marketing the property as hunting, farming or recreational land.**

20. b. While building structures can add value, it's important to bear in mind that doing so **may add to the costs of property taxes,** as it can move your property from an unimproved category to an improved category.

21. Consider select cutting timber from the property. Timber can be **select cut...don't clear cut...**and will likely not be noticed by buyers. My father, after buying his retirement property, select cut timber and recouped twenty percent of his

land costs...it was hardly noticeable. Just make sure you hire someone who will be sensitive to existing trees, views, and your future sell potential.

22. Create Physical Access. Ideally, you will also want to have a driveway, either asphalt or gravel, to **access the entire property.** Or, just a well-marked trail to the backside of the property could be acceptable on some properties.

23. Add Curb appeal. It doesn't just apply to properties with homes. Improving the land's appearance is one simple way to boost the value of the property. Depending on the size of the property, this is a task that you can likely take on yourself.

Walk through your property, and **make note of things that you can improve**, such as:

* Removing junk and garbage

* Clearing overgrown shrubs

* Pruning trees

* Pull weeds

* Clear brush

* Remove environmental hazards, such as unused wells or chemicals...just make sure you follow governmental rules and regulations.

24. Add Fencing. Fencing will almost always enhance the value of land. It should be installed in accordance with what the land is used for. A white board horse fence is not appropriate for a large cattle operation, but it's perfect for the showy horse farm. Conversely, a well-stretched, well stayed, barbed wire fence will be positively appealing to a cattleman.

Fencing **can accomplish several objectives at once**, and different types of fencing are used for specific applications. A fence can define the perimeter of the land, contain livestock, or keep unwanted animals out. A cross fence can keep livestock off of farm ground or provide efficient use of pastures. A yard fence can protect valuable landscaping and add interest and beauty to the yard area. A high deer fence can protect orchards, ornamental trees, vegetable gardens, and flowers.

No matter which type or types of fencing is used, it should be well-maintained, and the maintenance cost and time factor should be considered when choosing it.

25. Create a Farm or Tree Farm. If you own farmland, utilizing it will definitely increase its value. Not only will the crop bring in cash, but **it will also increase the eye appeal.** If you do not have the time and capability to farm, there are usually neighbor farmers who will operate the farm on a lease or share basis. Your production records will provide proof to a buyer of the value of the land.

If you own timberland, you could actually decrease the value by not taking care of it. Trees sustain damage in a variety of ways, from diseases like root rot to insect damage, parasite vegetation, dry weather stress, snow breakage, and other causes. All of these leave your woods in a messy condition and often perpetuate problems. The forest can be managed to promote healthy tree growth, good wildlife habitat, plus recreational use. All of these will increase the value of your land.

If you are not familiar with good forestry practices, get together with a local forestry consultant. He or she will advise you on proper tree spacing for maximum tree nutrients and sun exposure, how to provide wildlife corridors, and how to treat or prevent insect and disease damage. It may be that you should thin your timber for optimum forest health. That may provide cash that you could use for future forest enhancement.

26. Build a Pond Few things can bring as much enjoyment as a small pond or lake. A well placed pond can **create views and provide for lots of recreational opportunities.** In most cases, you will need to obtain permits...and it can be a laborious task to do it. However, if you can get the permit, this can be a nice addition especially for someone looking for an estate property with horses and other animals.

27. Get Rid of a Pond What? Thought I just told you to build one? Well, I've also seen property very adversely affected when **beavers moved in** and created a water body. Remember, that when you, or beavers, create a water body, then additional buffers come into play. These buffers can affect future development and therefore decrease your value.

Stay ahead of the beavers and don't let them start building. If not, you could find yourself with government regulations reducing the development ability of your property. And, once a water body is established, you normally can't just "undo" it. So, be vigilant.

28. Add Wildlife Habitat. Even if you aren't a hunter, having abundant wildlife on your property is an advantage. Remember, in many ways, if you are selling land, then **you're selling a way of life**...a reprieve from the city life. Seeing a big 8-point buck grazing in a green field of rye grass or seeing a spring turkey strutting along a wooded path, adds to that mystique. When you can, plant food plots and thick cover areas to attract and keep wildlife. Check with your state wildlife agency, or extension service, for more ways to enhance native plant species, attract wildlife, and establish wildlife habitat management plans.

29. Prepare a Building Pad for a Proposed home or building locations.

If your property has an obvious location for buildings, then go ahead and **clear the site of trees and shrubs.** Make sure you follow local regulations and soil erosion mitigation techniques, such as silt fence and temporary grassing.

30. Strategically locate wells.

In most jurisdictions, houses or septic systems **can not be located within certain distances of wells.** So, be careful where you locate a well; it can have consequences on locations of future homes.

31. Strategically locate septic tanks.

So, conversely, be careful of where you locate septic systems. **Their location can limit** where you place a well.

32. Never Give up a Well location.

Because of these distance requirements

mentioned previously, keep any wells that you have, even if they aren't in use.

It can help "protect" your property lines from development happening close to the wells from neighboring property and close to your property lines.

33. Consider running utilities to your property. Although this can be a

costly venture in some cases, having utilities in place will increase the value of your land significantly. For buyers, **properties with utilities are the ideal choice.**

If your property is located within city limits or in an established suburb, running utilities may be as simple as connecting to lines on the street and paying for hookup fees. However, if your property is located in a rural area, it will require more time, planning and money.

In this case, you may be required to obtain permits, get a percolation test, drill a well, install a septic tank, and pay to have electricity lines run. Although this can be a daunting, costly task, it will be a worthwhile investment if you own property in a desirable location.

Before you make the decision to run utilities to your property, sit down and determine whether it will be a worthwhile endeavor. Even if it adds 20% of the value of your land, the value increase may not be enough to cover the cost of running utility lines. You may also consider alternatives, such as solar or wind to provide power. A septic or well may also be more cost effective than connecting to city water or sewer lines.

34. Carefully consider Billboards & Cell Tower locations.
These types of uses can be a great asset or a great deterrent to development. **They can produce a nice income** for property that might have little value otherwise. However, I've also seen the "unattractiveness" of them reduce the value...substantially, of remaining property. In one case, our client has a cell tower that's not even being used anymore on his property. However, he can't entice the owner of the tower to agree to its removal. Subsequently, his land value

is at least half of what it would be without
the tower in place.

Legal & Tax Stuff

35. Fix Encroachments before the sale.
No one wants to buy your problem. And, few folks want to tackle dealing with a tough encroachment issue with a neighbor that they don't know. If you are aware of an encroachment issue, **go ahead and get it legally resolved with your neighbor** prior to putting the property on the market.   It may require hiring a surveyor or an attorney to figure it out.

36. Address Boundary Line Disputes asap.
Another potential hiccup is boundary line disputes. Fuzzy memories and old, incorrect surveys can sometimes cause some tense moments between neighbors.

It might behoove a seller to hire a surveyor help to figure out the situation. He can flag the corners, as well as the property line every 200 or 300 feet, depending on the size of the property. If you pretend there's not a problem, the buyer will probably eventually discover it, and the deal could go south.

37. Try Conservation Easements

Have you heard about conservation easements? If you own a sizable chunk of land, this recently approved little beauty is worth knowing about. Not only does it create some value, but also allows you to protect your land permanently for future generations. It is NOT to be confused with a county conservation easement designation.

The US Congress approved the use of this permanent easement recently. As a property owner, you are allowed to place your property in a permanent conservation easement with a qualified group...usually a Land Trust. **You retain title to the property, but the Land Trust maintains a permanent easement on the property.** That means you can't develop the property...forever. But, you retain title to the property. You still get to farm it and use it.

Why would you do this you might ask? Well, as a property owner, the difference in what you paid for the property and what it is appraised at, is X amount of value. That X amount of value can be a charitable contribution to the Land Trust. An investor can then take X as a tax write off over the next 16 years (the year of the contribution plus 15 years) If that investor has a $200,000 adjusted gross income, then they can write off $100,000 per year for the next 16 years until they reach that X amount.

In Georgia, as in a few other states, that X value can be sold to a taxpayer (investor) and then the title to the property can also be sold. If the math adds up, then you might be able to make some money on the property but preserve the land for generations to come. What could be better than that?

38. Are there any covenants or deed restrictions on the property to address?

I once passed up a great house on ten acres because the developer had placed a restriction against any animals, other than horses...no goats, chickens, no cute pot belly pigs, etc. We loved the house, but we were incensed that we couldn't have chickens. After all, even people in urban subdivisions are keeping chickens in their back yard now. If you have some odd restrictions like this on your property, **investigate with an attorney on removing them if possible.**

39. Don't give it all to Uncle Sam when you Sell. One of the concerns of selling your land is always the tax consequences.

I get it. Who wants to give money to the government when you don't have to? However, I have some strategies that can help.

One of those is in dealing with capital gains tax. Capital gains tax directly affects your exit strategy, and it's something that you must understand prior to selling a property. If you sell property that has been used as income producing, then you will owe what is called "capital gains tax." The tax can be divided into two categories:

1.   Depreciation deductions – 100% of the amount you deducted for depreciation while you owned it, will be taxed at 25%. Depreciation reduces your taxable income while you own it. However, depreciation reduces your "basis" in the property; and

therefore, increases the gain on the sale by an equal amount.

2.   Gain from appreciation – 100% of the amount is taxed up to a maximum of 20%.

Not really interested in paying this tax? Then you need to know that the IRS has created a way around paying it. It's called a 1031 exchange, like-kind exchange, or Starker exchange. The 1031 comes from the section of the IRS code that allows you to defer capital gains.

In 1970, a family named Starker challenged the IRS's ruling on capital gains and eventually won the court case against the IRS. A 1031 exchange merely allows you to swap properties without actually swapping the property.

When you sell an investment property, IRS rules will allow you to purchase a "like" property, of equal or greater value, and defer the capital gains into the new property. A third party company, known as an exchange intermediary, that's approved by the IRS, will hold your funds from the sale of the first property until you are able to close on the second property. If done properly, this "exchange" will allow you to defer the capital gains until the sale, or another exchange, of this second property.

It is possible, upon your death, to bequeath the property, and your heirs will not have to pay capital gains either. In effect, through the use of the 1031 exchange, it is possible never to pay capital gains in your lifetime. Who says you can't cheat the taxman?

While you may do whatever you can to avoid paying this tax, you will probably need to do the math to see if it actually makes sense. Right now, capital gains tax is 20%. Plus, a 3.8% medicare surtax (from the Affordable Care Act) on investment income will apply.

Depending upon your tax situation, it may make sense to bite the bullet and pay the tax anyway. I've had properties that I had huge capital expenditures on; but after calculating the intermediary's fees, I decided it best to just pay the tax and move on. Other properties have had a sizable capital gains tax, so I preferred to defer the capital gains by purchasing another property.

One thing to keep in mind is that there is a time limit on finding a property to purchase. Many investors have made dumb mistakes because of this time limit. They purchase something that is overpriced, or they buy a property without performing proper due diligence. Many sellers salivate when they hear that a 1031 investor is looking at their property. They know that someone under a time crunch and determined not to pay a capital gains tax will do some pretty dumb stuff. If you find yourself in a 1031 exchange, keep it quiet when you are looking for properties to purchase.

40. Create Legal Access. If your
property doesn't have road access and you don't already have a formal agreement in place, it may be time to speak to your neighbor about creating a legal easement. It's relatively simple and inexpensive to **create an easement and road maintenance agreement,** but be sure to consult with the title company and a real estate agent to ensure that your agreement is legally binding. Land can be difficult or impossible to sell if it has no access, and will diminish the value of your property significantly.

41. Be sure all Owners are Committed.

There's usually one person in every group that likes to flex his muscles...proving he knows more about a transaction than the rest. He's usually the one that throws a wrench in the deal at the last minute. So, we recommend you **obtain a limited power of attorney from all the owners** prior to marketing the property, unless you are absolutely on the same page, as with a spouse. This will ensure one person has the right to make the decision for the entire group and there aren't any last minute hiccups.

42. Be Sure Sentimental Value doesn't Stop the sale.

Land certainly has sentimental value to the seller. But, it has nothing but market value for the buyer. **Therein lies the rub for some land deals.** We all like to leave something for the grandchildren. But, I've seen so many kids and grandkids sell the land as soon as they inherit it...and that can create all kinds of estate and probate issues...as well as can cause discord amongst the heirs. What might have lots of sentimental value to the seller, may having nothing but monetary value to their heirs. It might be better to sell now, and gift the cash to your heirs, so they don't squabble over your life long investment.

43. Consider Assembling Your Property with Others.
When it comes to developing, sometimes bigger is better. The developer reduces his costs per unit (or per square foot in the case of commercial), which allows him to reduce costs to his end customer...and also increase his profits. I've had many smaller land deals refused by developers because of that very reason. Everyone only has so much time in a work week to look at deals, so a developer wants to focus on the ones that make him the biggest percentage profit. **Smaller land deals take up as much time as a large deal but produce less profit.** So, ask your neighbors if they will join you.

Marketing & Advertising

44. Talk to some appraisers. They will know some of the biggest names in the business and which investors are currently buying properties. **They also might give you some ideas on valuations.** It would also be beneficial to hire one to give you a professional opinion of value.

45. Call some of the well-known investors and property owners in your market. Give them your personal attention, tell them that you have some great opportunities (with regard to the property you're trying to sell). You also can contact the local municipality to determine some of the larger landowners in your area. **Give them a call or drop them a note.**

46. Contact the local economic development director or planning

director. Many of the local government officials talk with developers and buyers. **They also receive calls** from out of town businesses looking to start up in the area. They can be good resources for those types of buyers.

47. Join a local REIA (real estate investor's association) and

announce your property to all of the investors who attend. At one time, Georgia had the largest REIA in the nation. **Membership is usually inexpensive** but very valuable.

48. Talk to some Mortgage Brokers and use their various buyer

connections in your market. Ask if they will put your property on their email newsletter. Many of them keep clients on their email blasts list for many years, and they can have **hundreds of potential buyers.** Promise to work with them if a sell happens.

49. Talk to some hard money lenders

and leverage their various connections in your area. Hard money lenders typically lend on properties that banks won't. So, their leads probably won't be able to get financing, but they work in the world of finding really good deals and financing at 65% loan to value ratios (which means they usually have 35% down payment cash). Their buyers are also used to paying very expensive interest rates and origination points, which means **you might be able to undercut their usual deals** (if you are willing to owner finance). And, they have cash to get the deal done.

50. Call some local home builders

and see if they are looking for any buying opportunities. Look especially for those whose sales are strong. Look for those whose prices are going up. **Stop in and talk with their on-site sales agents** to see how sales are going and get contact info of who to talk to.

51. Visit some real estate auctions (also see #84) (tax sales, foreclosure

auctions, etc.). These places tend to be saturated with **cash buyers**.

Tell them about your property for sale. You could have buyers lining up to buy your property if you're actually offering a good deal.

52. Send out letters to the surrounding property owners. You can pull list from internet services of everyone with 2 or 3 miles of your location. **It's inexpensive** and works quite often.

53. Advertise your property in a Classified Newspaper Ad or craigslist. As a real estate professional, I use craigslist and obtain some pretty good activity off of it. **Make sure you use an aerial picture.** You can get one from Google maps.

54. Offer to finance the purchase of your land. One difficulty buyers experience when purchasing land is obtaining financing. Offering seller-carried financing for your land will create a larger

pool of potential buyers. **Plus, you'll get to a sale quicker.** You don't have to wait on bank red tape and appraisals. It's just you and the buyer.

55. Be creative with the down payment.
Consider financing buyers with little or no down payment as well. If a buyer can afford your monthly financing payments but doesn't have enough for a large down payment, consider offering financing along with a minimal down payment. I've even sold properties with the buyer not coming up with a down payment until many months after the closing. **Listen to the buyer** to see what REALLY works for them...not what just works for you.

56. Contact potential land buyers directly
to see if they're interested in your property. Neighbors or contractors who are building houses in the area might be prime potential buyers for your land. **Neighbors are the best source by far.** I've had at least five friends tell me that they want to buy my neighbor's property if it ever goes on the market. And, I keep an eye on them,

because most people want to live near friends.

57. Put a "FOR SALE" sign in the yard. Why do you think real estate agents do this? Because it works. **Many of my sales come from this simple task.** Generally, people that are driving by are the ones that will become buyers.

58. Create your own website and list your property for the world to see. I do this for many of my larger properties...**especially if there's something really unique** about the property or it's in a unique area. We recently created a website just for one tract of land on Lake Lanier...showing the virtues of Lake Lanier life. It's driven some buyers to look at the property where they might have passed over it before.

59. Try some website services, such as Zillow and Land and Farm. These sites **reach millions of buyers** all over the

world. We use a lot of these websites when we are marketing properties. The more eyes that see it...the more buyers...and the more you'll get for the property. I use the example of having a garage sale. If you have an item to sell, is it easier to sell by sticking it out on the driveway during a garage sale or placing it on eBay for all the world to see? Few people will see it on the driveway. Thousands will see it on eBay.

60. Use Pay Per Click mediums

like Google Adwords or Facebook posts. These work as **you can specifically target age groups and persons with interest in your area**. You can even target people within a certain mile radius of your property. It's some of the best advertising bangs for your buck.

61. Create Banner Ads and pay for

direct advertising on **relevant** websites.

62. List your property on a paid

website. You can google some of these. Loopnet is a good one. Land and Farm.

Commercial Search. **They change constantly,** so keep up to date.

63. Join some Real Estate Investor forums. You can even **create your own group** on LinkedIn.

64. Talk to some property management companies in your area. These people work with dozens of hungry investors and have tons of local connections. Mention that you would be willing to **pay a referral fee.**

65. Subscribe to Real Estate Blogs. Read what other people are saying about land sales. Comment and occasionally **offer information** on your own property. But, be careful here. Most blogs don't take kindly to commercialization. You need to actually involve yourself in the discussion. Otherwise, they might ban you from participating if it's obvious you are just trying to sell something.

66. Talk to your title company and/or closing attorney. See if they know of any buyers who are actively looking for new investment properties. **They deal with buyers all day long,** and likely many of them are friends.

67. Talk to some building inspectors – they often deal with some of the highest volume buyers and sellers in your market. And, **they are generally knowledgeable about properties.** Typically, they won't be abreast on values, but they can put you in touch with the people that are.

68. Place magnetic signs and window stickers on your car. Wherever you drive, let people know you've got some great deals available. If you live in a populated area, this **can generate thousands** of views per day. Make sure it's easy to read going down the road. Just include 3 or 4 words plus your phone number or website.

69. Place small bandit signs in

several areas around town...with "land for sale", acreage and a phone number. Just make sure you **follow the local rules** and regulations on placing signage.

70. Post your business cards and/or brochures on some local

bulletin boards (laundry mats, hardware stores, farm supply stores, restaurants, salons, college campuses, schools, etc.). **Target places** where people have some free time or where landowners/buyers shop.

71. Geo Fencing advertising is a

superb investment. This is usually done in conjunction with billboard advertising...and most billboard companies offer this service now. You can target any demographic of people, any age group, etc., within a certain mile radius of any location. When they open a cell phone app, your banner ad can appear on their screen. They then click this ad, and it goes to a website splash page. One company I know of has the ability to advertise within 45,000 cell phone apps! This is very directed marketing and hence more expensive than most. But, it **gets your message out to a targeted audience.**

72. Distribute flyers wherever buyers congregate (REIA's, Real estate seminars, Chambers of Commerce, Trade Shows, etc.) **Make the flyers very professional**.

You might try the website, Fiverr, or similar websites to have a professional flyer designed for less than a sit-down restaurant meal.

73. Public Speaking. Let the world know about your properties through public speaking engagements. I know most people fear this more than death.

But, you can **memorize a short 30 second** "elevator speech" to deliver at networking events, church events, chamber gatherings, etc....it probably won't kill you.

74. Google "We Buy Houses" and then "Your City/County" to find property buyers

in your area. **Use Google a lot.** You'd be surprised what resources are available on the internet.

75. Search "Real Estate Investor"

on **Facebook**, **Twitter** and **LinkedIn** to find anyone in your area who has this **listed as their job title.** Communicate with them to see if they have any buyers for your property.

76. Create a Direct Mail

Campaign. Using internet searches, you can find a list of all the **properties in your area that have sold** over the past 6 – 24 months. From this list, create a direct mail campaign to let these people know that you have some great deals on real estate and that you're looking for investors who want to buy them.

77. Keep an eye out for the "For

Rent" signs in your area. Reach out to these owners with a simple letter or phone call. They usually have more than one property and **might be looking to purchase more**. I've purchased several really good deals this way, and you will be able to find investors using this method as well.

78. Create a short video showcasing your property and post it on YouTube. **Keep it under two minutes.** Otherwise, a viewer will get bored before they finish it. I've done this for years. It's free advertising. And websites like youtube are surpassing many traditional search engines in popularity. You might want to use a throwaway phone number; though, as you could receive calls for years after you post the video and after you've already sold the property.

79. Lease a billboard to advertise your property. This may sound expensive, and it can be, but it could be worth your while to **find a qualified buyer**. Place it as close to your property as possible. In some rural areas, a billboard can be leased for just several hundred bucks per month...not a bad investment for some great exposure.

80. Hire a land planner to create a

conceptual sketch. You'll need to locate a professional such as a landscape architect or civil engineer. Most importantly, use someone with experience in your type of land and what kind of development might be proposed on it and with the jurisdiction in which your property is located. Also, **make sure they have some good graphic skills**, to showcase the proposed plan. It needs to be to-scale and color rendered for best effect.

81. Buy a large color ad in your local newspaper, using this **color-rendered plan that the land planner prepared.** Many land buyers, who tend to be older, are avid newspaper readers.

82. Use aerial photos when

possible. A picture from your car window normally doesn't work for land deals. So, **use an aerial and outline the property line.** You can get aerial photos from Google Earth or your local government's GIS website...just google "Your County" and "GIS."

83. Hire a drone operator for a cool video shot. Drones are getting cheaper and cheaper, which means finding someone to shoot some drone video is getting very affordable. Hire them to **create a video and post it on Youtube.** They can then give you a link that you can email to potential buyers.

84. Auction the property if you must. So, I've reluctantly added this as a tip to **sell land fast. I DON'T think it will generate higher profits** for several reasons. Number one, auction buyers are expecting to get a steal. They are usually sophisticated, and the odds of getting them "caught up in the moment" are pretty slim. So, you've got a sophisticated buyer going shopping for a steal of a deal...not the situation you want to be in. Secondly, few auctions pay little in the way of real estate commissions to a real estate agent representing the buyer...the auctioneer gets the lion's share of the commission. That means real estate agents with buyers seldom attend. And those two issues combined mean less money for the seller...but, it will be fast.

85. Use field Cameras to get Pictures of Your Wildlife. You can

buy a field camera for less than $40. Attach it to a tree, and it automatically takes pictures or videos when it's motion activated. **Use this to document all the wildlife** on your property. Use the pictures in your marketing to buyers.

86. Find a Topography Map of the property. You can usually get these at

your County Zoning office or on their GIS system (which is usually online and available to the public). In some instances, this may not be available, and you may have to hire a surveyor to prepare one.

You should ask for contour lines of 2' minimum for smaller tracts and 5' for larger tracts. **Provide these to a buyer as part of your marketing package**.

87. Have a Surveyor Locate Floodplain Areas. Your marketing

package should also include 100 year floodplain areas. While you normally can't build within this area, it doesn't mean floodplain has no value. Most jurisdictions allow floodplain to be credited toward overall density...**which helps to increase your overall value.** Of course, land is more valuable if it's all buildable, but floodplain is not an entirely lost cause.

88. Investigate surrounding properties. Are you located next to
someone with junk cars in the yard? A property with old junky mobile homes? If so, you might **want to consider buying those properties just to clean up the area.** It could be an expensive fix but could pay off by getting you a higher sales price on both tracts after the clean-up.

Brokers & Pricing

89. How Long do you Want to take to Sell? In general, pricing drives the length of any sale. **Price it well below market, and your land will go quickly.** Price it well above market, and it will sit there a long time. I know it's common sense, but it needs to be said. I usually recommend a seller to consider a six-month price, 12-month price, and 24-month price. Six months is below market, 12 months is at market, and 24-months is slightly above market. Of course, timing can be greatly affected by the need for rezoning and availability of transportation and sewer...among other things.

90. Call other Real Estate Agents
and ask if they know of any buyers. If you have it listed with a real estate company, you will want to **forego this tactic** as it is frowned upon in the professional community. But, if you are going it alone, give it a shot.

91. Bring coffee & donuts into your local realtor's office. Tell the entire team that you'll **pay them a referral fee** for any buyers they can send your way. You won't have to pay anything until you get to closing. However, you will open yourself up to some aggressive agents. So, be ready for the pressure. And, you will probably wind up listing with one of them if you don't sell it yourself...which is not a bad thing.

92. Evaluate the local market conditions for land similar to yours. Pricing your land correctly is one key in selling it fast. But before you can price your land, you need an objective understanding of what has been selling in the past six months as well as how your land compares. **A good real estate agent can help you with this.** Or, you can hire an appraiser to help you determine the value.

93. Underprice your land and set the price below the current average of recent sales. This strategy differs from pricing your land according to current market

levels. If in the past six months, land similar to yours has sold for an average of $50,000 per acre, but current listings are at $75,000, listing your land below $50,000 will help **generate a quicker sale** than listing it at $60,000.

94. List your land with a real estate broker specializing in land sales.

Of course, you can sell it yourself. But, can you get it in front of as many buyers as a qualified broker can? No. He has dozen of websites that he pays for. And, if he's good at his job, he has an email database of thousands of potential customers...ours is topping 15,000, and we add more every day of the week. Remember, **a broker also deals with buyers every day.** He probably has other property listings that buyers are calling on. People stop him in the grocery store and at church to talk about real estate. It's a full-time job for him. And, having that full-time broker will pay off for you in the long run by finding more potential buyers; and logically, someone who is willing to pay more for your land.

95. If it's been on the market awhile, try a new company.

Or, if you've had it for sale by owner, try a real estate company. Because of the **"nobody wants a deal that nobody else wants"** phenomenon, you need to change things up occasionally. Just new signage with different colors and different marketing could make the difference.

96. Seriously Consider the First Offer.

There's an old saying in real estate, **"the first offer is the best."** There is a lot of truth to that. Nobody wants a deal that nobody else wants. If the property has been on the market for too long, buyers start wondering what's wrong with it. And, they subconsciously, or consciously, start discounting the price for this "imagined" flaw. I've seen so many sellers accept deals months later at 20-30% below their original offer, because of this. Try to make the first offer work, if you can.

97. Pay an above Market Real Estate Commission.

Larger

commissions provide incentives to real estate agents to move quickly and to put in extra work in on marketing and selling your land as rapidly as possible. Ok, I know I'm biased here. But, it really works. **People always work harder on deals that pay them more.** It's just human nature. And, the harder your agent works, the more buyers will see it, and the higher price you will receive for your property.

98. Don't hire a Part Time Agent.

Real estate is a full-time job. There's no way around it. **Would you hire a doctor that's part time? Do you want your mechanic to be part time?** Why would you hire a real estate broker that's not full time? A good agent lives and breathes real estate. It's not unusual for a good commercial agent to work 70 hours per week. The more you work at anything, the better you are at it. A good agent is talking to everyone about real estate. It's his passion. He's attending parties and talking about real estate. He reads commercial real estate magazines and newsletters. He studies it day and night. He knows the market, knows the key players in town, and knows buyers. He even writes about real estate...like I do. He's on top of his game. If he's playing two games, he can't be on the top of either one.

99. Verify that your Agent is full-time.
With the internet these days, it's hard to hide from the truth. Google your agent's name. Look through the first three or four pages of results. If you don't see his name as it relates to your type of property, then he's either not full time or not very active, or successful.

Go to www.Linkedin.com and see if he has a professional profile there. Most of these guys aren't very good at hiding their tracks. **They'll straddle the fence on their day job and their real estate job because they're just not sure which one they want to do, or aren't successful at either one**. Many will still have a LinkedIn account announcing that to the world.

When you are interviewing him, make sure you set up the appointment during the work day. Watch out for lunch time. Make sure it's during the time he would have to be at work if he had a full-time job.

And, don't give him too much time to schedule it. If you want to be really sneaky, set an appointment for one of these times, cancel and request another appointment for a similar time. See how flexible he is. If he only wants to meet after 5:00 pm, during the week, or on Saturday, run the other way. That means he's working a full-time job and giving you his second best!

100. Land sells take patience. Most residential agents are accustomed to a closing happening in 30 days. Land closings can take a year or more. So, residential agents aren't set up for that kind of closings...mentally, or financially. I have seen **sellers accept low ball offers because of pressure from their "residential agent."** It's human nature. Their agent "needs" a quick sale, so they pressure the seller. You don't want to be in that situation.

101. Verify that your Agent Actually sells Land.

This is the **biggest mistake** I see in selling land; hence, I saved it for last. Someone will hire their friend who's sold a few houses in the past...or someone from church that "does real estate." I guess they assume all real estate is the same. **Not true at all.** Land listings should be marketed totally different than homes...totally different buyers, different listing platforms, different contracts, different expectations, different problems to deal with, and different players in the process. If you want to waste time, hire one of those folks. **If you want to sell the property, and increase your moo-la, hire an expert.**

ABOUT THE AUTHOR

Brian Patton's experience has included land planning large scale master planned golf communities throughout the United States and foreign countries, land planning mixed use commercial developments in the Atlanta Region, and brokering office, retail, restaurant, and land deals in the state of Georgia.

Included with this experience were several years of developing site plans for commercial, industrial and residential developments.

A stint in the public sector as a city planner and zoning administrator, as well as zoning and development consulting work, has afforded Mr. Patton a distinct knowledge of the governmental approval and development process.

Brian has been a columnist on real estate issues in seven different newspapers with a weekly copy circulation of 120,000+. His books have been taught in major Universities in the Southeast.

Additionally, he has taught numerous real estate courses, is a past guest with GA Reia, the largest real estate investors association in the country, and he just finished up a two-year stint as the co-host of a weekly radio show on real estate.

Mr. Patton obtained his Registered Land Planning / Landscape Architecture status in 1993 and his Real Estate licensure in 1993. His designation as a CCIM came in early 2002.

He shares his experiences in land sales with readers of this book in hopes that they can turn their land deals into their own "cash cow."

Contact the author:

Brian Patton, CCIM

(770) 634-4848

www.BrianPattonLand.com